THE LEARNING RESOURCE CENTER
Weston Intermediate School

POETRY BASICS

○

CONCRETE POETRY

○

VALERIE BODDEN

CREATIVE ❦ EDUCATION

Published by Creative Education
P.O. Box 227, Mankato, Minnesota 56002
Creative Education is an imprint of The Creative Company
www.thecreativecompany.us

Design and production by Stephanie Blumenthal
Printed by Corporate Graphics in the United States of America

Photographs by Alamy (INTERFOTO Pressebildagentur), Guillaume Apollinaire, Art Resource (Digital
Image © The Museum of Modern Art/ Licensed by SCALA, Jenny Holzer Studio), Baurenfeid, The
Bridgeman Art Library (Guillaume Apollinaire), Corbis (Blue Lantern Studio, Roger Wood), Getty Images
(Jay Belmore), The Granger Collection, New York; © Nachlass Ball-Hennings, Robert Walser-Archiv Zürich

Typographic interpretation of Eugene Ionesco's *The Bald Soprano*, by Massin,
photography copyright © 2009 Henry Cohen (cover and 1)

Graphic interpretation by Massin, copyright © 2009 Massin (3)

The image on page 5 first appeared in *The Arte of English Poesie*, by George Puttenham,
published in London in 1589 by Richard Field. Reprinted by permission of Kent State University Press.

Images on pages 11 and 27 © 2009 Jenny Holzer, member Artists Rights Society (ARS), New York
Image by Winterhouse, copyright © 2007 Poetry Foundation (30)

Library of Congress Cataloging-in-Publication Data
Bodden, Valerie.
Concrete poetry / by Valerie Bodden.
p. cm. — (Poetry basics)
Includes bibliographical references and index.
ISBN 978-1-58341-775-1
1. Concrete poetry—History and criticism—Juvenile literature. I. Title. II. Series.

PN1455.B55 2009
809.1'4—dc22   2008009156
C.1
6 8 9 7

People have written poems for thousands of years. Long ago, when people wanted to tell a story, they made it into a poem. Today, people write poems about all kinds of topics, from sunsets to traffic jams. Poems can help readers see things in a new way. They can make readers laugh or cry, sigh or scream. The goal of the type of poetry known as concrete is to have the shape or appearance of a poem reflect what the words express.

CONCRETE FOUNDATIONS

The origins of concrete poetry reach far back into history. More than 2,000 years ago, writers in ancient Greece created pattern, or shaped, poems. The words in these poems were arranged to take the shapes of different objects. The Greeks may have been following examples they had seen from even earlier works created in India and Persia (present-day Iran).

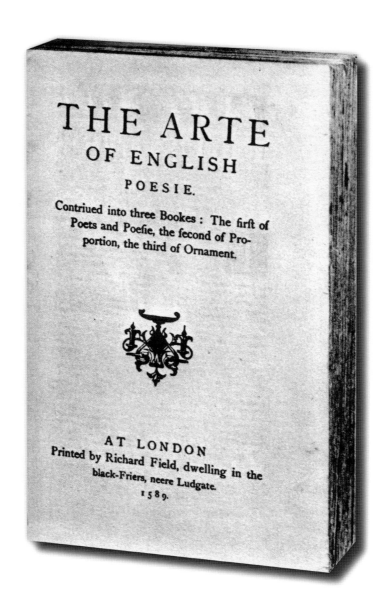

During the 1400s and 1500s, a few poets in Europe who had been introduced to Greek pattern poetry began to experiment with the form. Then, in 1589, *The Arte of English Poesie* was published in England. An entire chapter of the book was devoted to pattern poetry.

George Herbert

The publication of this book led to a surge in the popularity of pattern poetry across England. Many of the English poems were religious in nature and took the shape of angels' wings or an altar (a raised table used for religious ceremonies). The poem on the opposite page by 17th-century English poet George Herbert is an example of an altar-shaped poem.

A BROKEN ALTAR, Lord, thy servant rears,
Made of a heart and cemented with tears;
Whose parts are as thy hand did frame;
No workman's tool hath touch'd the same.
                    A HEART alone
                    Is such a stone
                    As nothing but
                    Thy pow'r doth cut.
                    Wherefore each part
                    Of my hard heart
                    Meets in this frame
                    To praise thy name;
That if I chance to hold my peace,
These stones to praise thee may not cease.
O let thy blessed SACRIFICE be mine,
And sanctify this ALTAR to be thine.

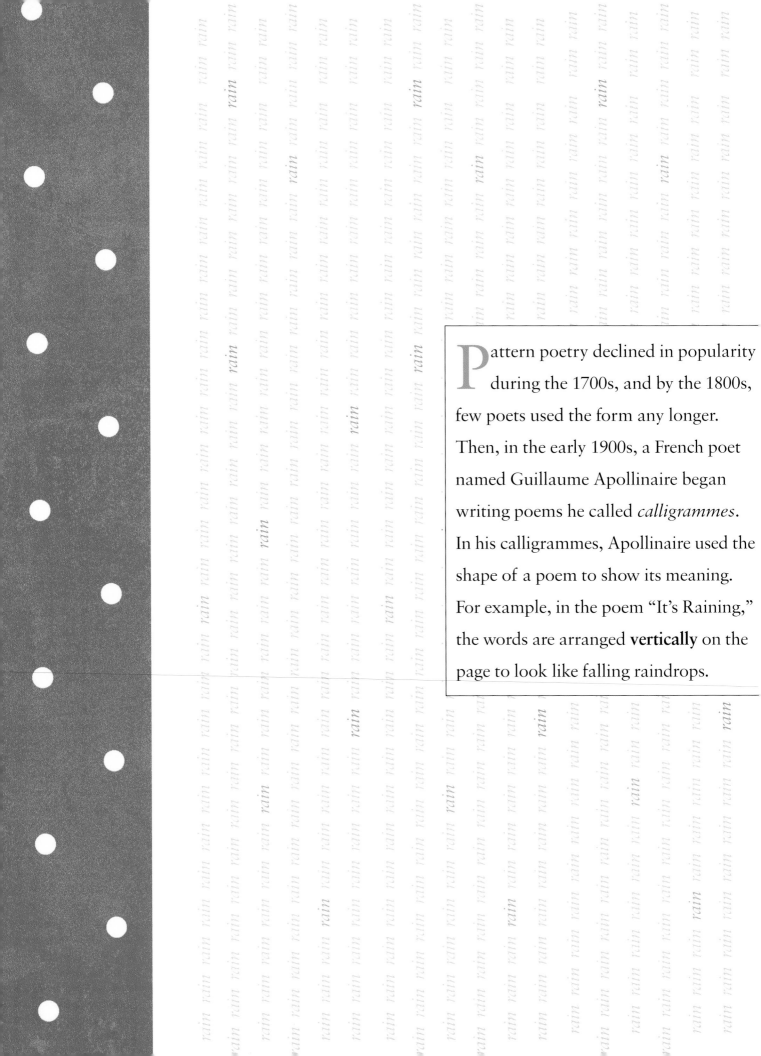

Pattern poetry declined in popularity during the 1700s, and by the 1800s, few poets used the form any longer. Then, in the early 1900s, a French poet named Guillaume Apollinaire began writing poems he called *calligrammes*. In his calligrammes, Apollinaire used the shape of a poem to show its meaning. For example, in the poem "It's Raining," the words are arranged **vertically** on the page to look like falling raindrops.

Ab
capipe
T'en fais pas
HECTOR
LE PORION

Guillaume Apollinaire

By the 1950s, many poets were looking for new ways to write poetry. In Switzerland, Eugen Gomringer began to write what he called "constellations." In these poems, the words didn't necessarily take a shape, but the way the words were arranged was as important as what they said. At the same time, a group of poets in Brazil began to write similar pieces. In 1955, they gave the name "concrete poetry" to their work.

Eugen Gomringer

Soon, the concrete poetry movement had spread across the world. Although it reached the height of its popularity in the 1960s, concrete poetry is still written by poets today. Some have even made **animated** concrete poems on the Internet!

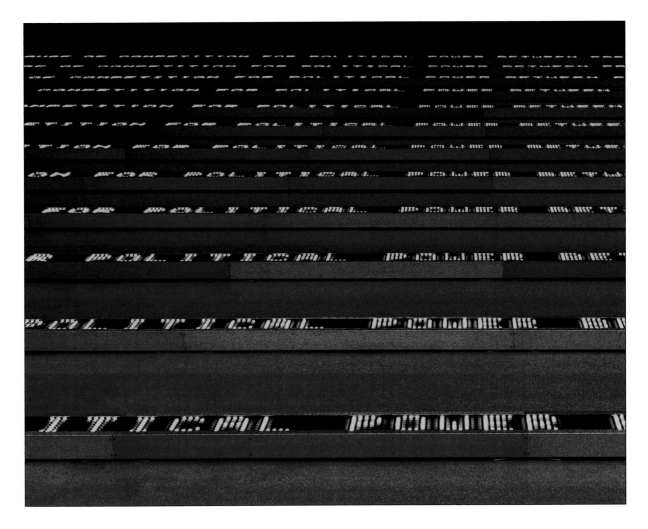

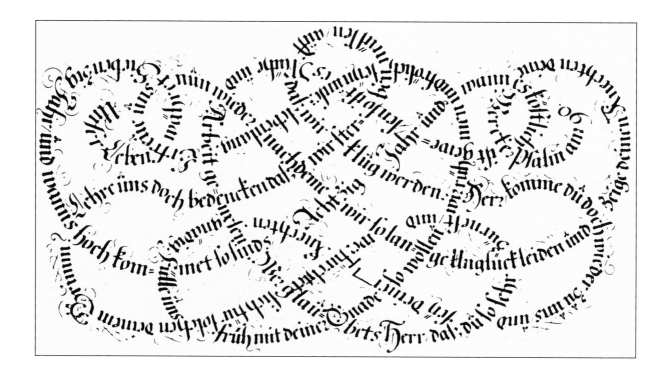

Most concrete poems probably do not look like the type of poetry you are used to reading. Most traditional poems are made up of several lines that usually begin at or near the left **margin**. But in a pattern or concrete poem, the words can be anywhere on the page.

While most traditional poems are meant to be read, concrete poems are meant to be seen. Looking at a concrete poem can be almost like looking at a painting. In fact, if you try to read a concrete poem out loud, much of its meaning may be lost.

RENT

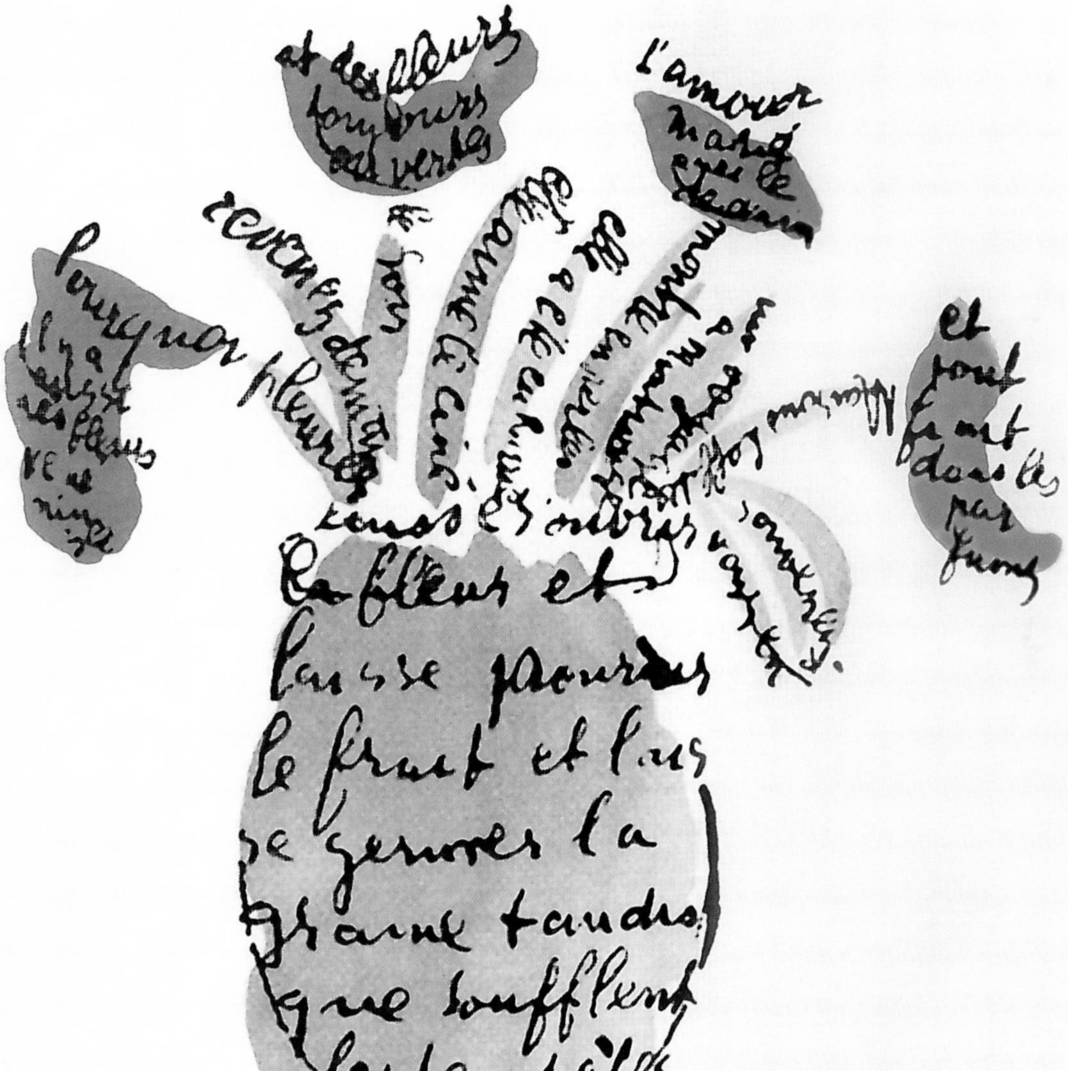

In many concrete poems, the structure of the poem creates an image of the poem's subject or idea. As you read "The Mouse's Tale" from English author Lewis Carroll's 1865 book *Alice's Adventures in Wonderland*, notice how the poem's shape is related to the ideas it presents. In this poem, "prosecute" means "bring to court," and "cur" means "mean dog."

"Fury said to
a mouse, That
he met in the
house, 'Let
us both go
to law: *I*
will prose-
cute *you*.—
Come, I'll
take no de-
nial: We
must have
the trial;
For really
this morn-
ing I've
nothing
to do.'
Said the
mouse to
the cur,
'Such a
trial, dear
Sir, With
no jury
or judge,
would
be wast-
ing our
breath.'
'I'll be
judge,
I'll be
jury,'
said
cun-
ning
old
Fury:
'I'll
try
the
whole
cause,
and
con-
demn
you to
death.'"

Some concrete poems do not form a shape. But the arrangement of the poem's words and letters is still important. In some concrete poems, words or letters are scattered across the page. In others, a single word in the middle of the page might serve as an entire poem.

word ONE

Sometimes, the same word might be repeated over and over but arranged in a unique way to make a point. For example, Eugen Gomringer deals with the subject of silence in a five-line poem. All of the lines except the third consist of the word *silencio* (Spanish for "silence") repeated three times. The third line has an empty space where the second *silencio* would be. The empty space in the middle of the poem helps to make its "silence" more real.

In addition to emphasizing the placement of words, concrete poets also sometimes change the **font** used for the words. A bold font may suggest something different from a squiggly one. The color of various words can also affect the overall meaning of a poem.

silencio silencio silencio
silencio silencio silencio
silencio   silencio
silencio silencio silencio
silencio silencio silencio

Lewis Carroll

Usually when you read a poem, the words of the poem create a picture of its meaning in your mind. This is true of some types of pattern or concrete poetry as well. George Herbert's altar-shaped poem on page 7 and Lewis Carroll's "The Mouse's Tale" on page 14 can be read much like traditional poems. If the poems were printed in traditional lines, they might lose some of their visual appeal, but they would keep much of their meaning.

18

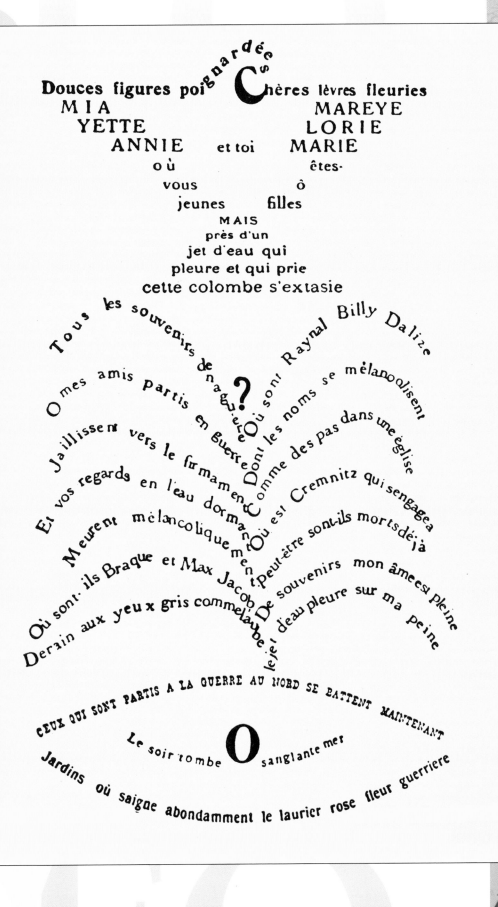

The subjects of these types of shaped poems can be almost anything that can take on a physical shape. Although **concrete** topics are usually easier to portray than **abstract** ideas, it is possible to create a concrete poem about feelings or ideas, too. For example, although "love" has no shape, the poem below gives it the shape of overlapping wedding rings. What other shapes do you think might have worked for this poem?

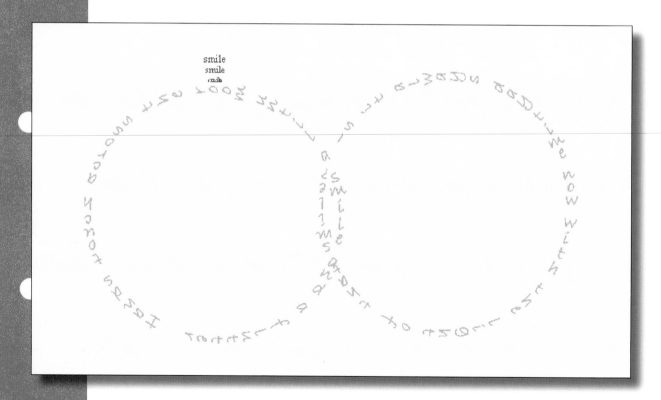

Even concrete poems that cannot be read out loud like traditional poetry often deal with the same subjects as other poems. Yet these types of poems treat their subjects in a completely different way. Instead of conveying their message through the use of descriptions or **imagery**, they communicate their message through the way words are arranged. These types of concrete poems usually cannot be understood unless they are seen. For example, the poem on the next page uses only two different words to illustrate its meaning. Although you can't "read" the poem in a traditional way, try to see if you can understand its meaning.

Because concrete poems are often so different from traditional types of poetry, they can sometimes be hard to understand. For example, it might take a while to figure out that the poem opposite is about loneliness. If the poem had been written in a traditional form and had described a situation in which a person was lonely, it might have been easier to understand. But it may not have had the same impact. Rather than telling you about loneliness, this poem attempts to show loneliness. In order to figure out the meaning of this kind of concrete poem, readers have to be actively involved in exploring and **interpreting** what they see in front of them.

ME

THEM THEM THEM
THEM THEM
THEM THEM
THEM THEM
THEM THEM THEM
THEM THEM THEM
THEM THEM THEM
THEM THEM THEM

Sometimes concrete poetry can be taken to even further extremes. For example, sound poetry focuses on sounds rather than on images. It is meant to be listened to like a song. Usually, sound poems do not consist of words at all but rather of made-up combinations of **syllables** or other noises (such as grunts) that the poet thinks sound good together.

Early 20th-century German poet Hugo Ball claimed that sound poems were "poetry without words." The poem at right is one of Ball's sound poems. Although the title of the poem, "Karawane," is German for "caravan," the rest of the words in the poem are not real words at all. Ball simply combined different letters for their sound effect. The different fonts used in the poem help to show how each line is to be read. Which lines do you think should be read with more force?

KARAWANE

jolifanto bambla ô falli bambla
grossiga m'pfa habla horem
égiga goramen
higo bloiko russula huju
hollaka hollala
anlogo bung
blago bung
blago bung
bosso fataka
ü üü ü
schampa wulla wussa ólobo
hej tatta gôrèm
eschige zunbada
wulubu ssubudu uluw ssubudu
tumba ba- umf
kusagauma
ba - umf

(1917)
Hugo Ball

Hugo Ball (opposite)

Other types of concrete poetry consist neither of words nor sounds. Instead, they are made up only of letters or **symbols**. These poems cannot be read or sounded out. They can only be seen. Sometimes, these types of poems form a shape or a pattern. The poem below is made up of only the letter "X." It cannot be read either quietly or out loud. If you had to give this poem a title, what would you call it?

While the poem on this page blurs the line between poetry and art, that line can be blurred even further by the inclusion of photographs in concrete poetry. For example, Brazilian poet Augusto de Campos composed a poem consisting of photographs of people's eyes arranged into a pyramid shape. Other concrete poets have continued to use words and symbols but have written them on objects rather than on paper. Some concrete poems have even been formed out of real concrete!

No matter where or how they are written, concrete poems are among the most unusual types of poems in the world. They break away from the structure—and often the meaning—of traditional poetry. But they are still poems. They still make you think, feel, and imagine. And after you've learned to interpret concrete poetry, you're sure to understand almost any kind of poem you encounter!

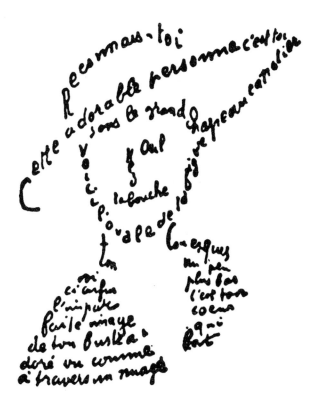

1. Taking shape. In order to write a shaped poem, first think of a topic that you would like to write about. Now decide what shape you could use to represent that topic. Draw an outline of your shape on a piece of paper, then write a poem to fill the shape. When you are done, rewrite your poem in a more traditional way, with lines beginning at the left margin. Which version do you like better?

2. Sound it out. Writing a sound poem gives you a chance to have fun with sounds. First, say some sounds (not words) out loud. Next, try to write those sounds down. For example, "shhaaaroom kala ba kala dabba." Type your sound poem, using different fonts to show how different parts of the poem should be read. When you are done, read your sound poem to your friends or family and ask how it makes them feel.

Burg, Brad. *Outside the Lines: Poetry at Play*. New York: G. P. Putnam's Sons, 2002.

Janeczko, Paul. *A Poke in the I: A Collection of Concrete Poems*. Cambridge, Mass.: Candlewick Press, 2001.

Lewis, J. Patrick. *Doodle Dandies: Poems That Take Shape*. New York: Atheneum Books for Young Readers, 1998.

Sidman, Joyce. *Meow Ruff: A Story in Concrete Poetry*. Boston: Houghton Mifflin, 2006.

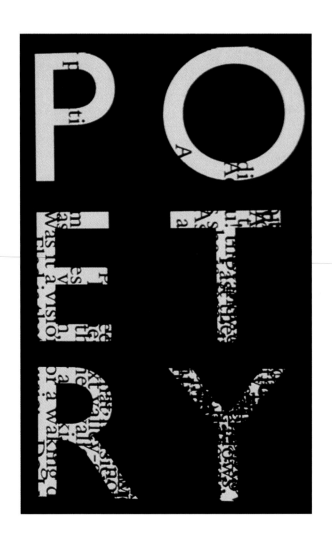

abstract—unable to be defined or described by the senses

animated—moving; in animated concrete poems on the Internet, the words move and change shape

concrete—able to be described by the senses

font—the specific size and style of printed letters and symbols

imagery—descriptive words that cause people to imagine what something looks like

interpreting—making sense of something or figuring out its meaning

margin—the blank space on each side of the printed words on a page

syllables—complete units of sound that make up words; for example "sit" has one syllable, and "si-lent" has two

symbols—printed signs that have a specific meaning; for example, the symbol "&" means "and"

vertically—upright; going up and down

BIBLIOGRAPHY

Cobbing, Bob, and Peter Mayer, comp. *Concerning Concrete Poetry*. London: Writers Forum, 1978.

Higgins, Dick. *George Herbert's Pattern Poems: In Their Tradition*. New York: Unpublished Editions, 1977.

Klonsky, Milton, ed. *Speaking Pictures: A Gallery of Pictorial Poetry from the Sixteenth Century to the Present*. New York: Harmony Books, 1975.

McGraw, H. Ward, ed. *Prose and Poetry for Enjoyment*. Chicago: L. W. Singer Co., 1935.

Newell, Kenneth. *Pattern Poetry: A Historical Critique from the Alexandrian Greeks to Dylan Thomas*. Boston: Marlborough House, 1976.

Solt, Mary Ellen, ed. *Concrete Poetry: A World View*. Bloomington, Ind.: Indiana University Press, 1970.